Highlights of GAO-10-338, a report to congressional requesters

March 2010

CYBERSECURITY

Progress Made but Challenges Remain in Defining and Coordinating the Comprehensive National Initiative

Why GAO Did This Study

In response to the ongoing threats to federal systems and operations posed by cyber attacks, President Bush established the Comprehensive National Cybersecurity Initiative (CNCI) in 2008. This initiative consists of a set of projects aimed at reducing vulnerabilities, protecting against intrusions, and anticipating future threats. GAO was asked to determine (1) what actions have been taken to develop interagency mechanisms to plan and coordinate CNCI activities and (2) what challenges CNCI faces in achieving its objectives related to securing federal information systems. To do this, GAO reviewed CNCI plans, policies, and other documentation and interviewed officials at the Office of Management and Budget (OMB), Department of Homeland Security, and the Office of the Director of National Intelligence (ODNI), among other agencies. GAO also reviewed studies examining aspects of federal cybersecurity and interviewed recognized cybersecurity experts.

What GAO Recommends

GAO is recommending that OMB take steps to address each of the identified challenges. OMB agreed with five of six recommendations, disagreeing with the recommendation regarding defining roles and responsibilities. However, such definitions are key to achieving CNCI's objective of securing federal systems.

View GAO-10-338 or key components.
For more information, contact Gregory C. Wilshusen at (202) 512-6244 or wilshuseng@gao.gov, or Davi D'Agostino at (202) 512-5431 or dagostinod@gao.gov.

What GAO Found

The White House and federal agencies have taken steps to plan and coordinate CNCI activities by establishing several interagency working groups. These include the National Cyber Study Group, which carried out initial brainstorming and information-gathering for the establishment of the initiative; the Communications Security and Cyber Policy Coordinating Committee, which presented final plans to the President and coordinated initial implementation activities; and the Joint Interagency Cyber Task Force, which serves as the focal point for monitoring and coordinating projects and enabling the participation of both intelligence-community and non-intelligence-community agencies. These groups have used a combination of status meetings and other reporting mechanisms to track implementation of projects.

CNCI faces several challenges in meeting its objectives:

- **Defining roles and responsibilities.** Federal agencies have overlapping and uncoordinated responsibilities for cybersecurity, and it is unclear where overall responsibility for coordination lies.
- **Establishing measures of effectiveness.** The initiative has not yet developed measures of the effectiveness in meeting its goals. While federal agencies have begun to develop effectiveness measures for information security, these have not been applied to the initiative.
- **Establishing an appropriate level of transparency.** Few of the elements of CNCI have been made public, and the rationale for classifying related information remains unclear, hindering coordination with private sector entities and accountability to the public.
- **Reaching agreement on the scope of educational efforts**. Stakeholders have yet to reach agreement on whether to address broad education and public awareness as part of the initiative, or remain focused on the federal cyber workforce.

Until these challenges are adequately addressed, there is a risk that CNCI will not fully achieve its goal to reduce vulnerabilities, protect against intrusions, and anticipate future threats against federal executive branch information systems.

The federal government also faces strategic challenges beyond the scope of CNCI in securing federal information systems:

- **Coordinating actions with international entities**. The federal government does not have a formal strategy for coordinating outreach to international partners for the purposes of standards setting, law enforcement, and information sharing.
- **Strategically addressing identity management and authentication.** Authenticating the identities of persons or systems seeking to access federal systems remains a significant governmentwide challenge. However, the federal government is still lacking a fully developed plan for implementation of identity management and authentication efforts.

Contents

Abbreviations

CNCI	Comprehensive National Cybersecurity Initiative
HSPD	Homeland Security Presidential Directive
NCSC	National Cyber Security Center
NSPD	National Security Presidential Directive
OMB	Office of Management and Budget
ODNI	Office of the Director of National Intelligence
OSTP	Office of Science and Technology Policy
US-CERT	U.S. Computer Emergency Readiness Team

United States Government Accountability Office
Washington, DC 20548

March 5, 2010

The Honorable Loretta Sanchez
Chairwoman
Subcommittee on Terrorism, Unconventional Threats and Capabilities
Committee on Armed Services
House of Representatives

The Honorable Adam Smith
House of Representatives

Pervasive and sustained cyber attacks against the United States continue to pose the threat of a potentially devastating impact on federal systems and operations. In January 2008, President Bush issued National Security Presidential Directive 54/Homeland Security Presidential Directive 23 (NSPD-54/HSPD-23), establishing the Comprehensive National Cybersecurity Initiative (CNCI), a set of projects aimed at safeguarding executive branch information systems by reducing potential vulnerabilities, protecting against intrusion attempts, and anticipating future threats. Shortly after taking office, President Obama, in February 2009, ordered a review of cybersecurity-related plans, programs, and activities underway throughout the federal government, including the CNCI projects. This review resulted in a May 2009 report that made recommendations for achieving a more reliable, resilient, and trustworthy digital infrastructure.

We were asked to determine (1) what actions have been taken to develop interagency mechanisms to plan and coordinate CNCI activities and (2) what challenges CNCI faces in achieving its objectives related to securing federal information systems. To do this, we analyzed CNCI plans and related agency documentation and interviewed officials at the Office of Management and Budget (OMB), the Department of Homeland Security (DHS), the Office of the Director of National Intelligence (ODNI), the Department of Justice, the Office of Science and Technology Policy (OSTP), the State Department, and the National Science Foundation. We also identified and reviewed recent studies, including GAO reports, that examined federal cybersecurity issues and interviewed agency officials and recognized cybersecurity experts.

On November 24, 2009, we briefed your staff on the results of our review. This report includes the materials used at the briefing, as well as the final recommendations we are making to the Director of OMB. The full briefing materials, including details on our scope and methodology, are reprinted in appendix I.

We conducted this performance audit from December 2008 to March 2010 in accordance with generally accepted government auditing standards. Those standards require that we plan and perform the audit to obtain sufficient, appropriate evidence to provide a reasonable basis for our findings and conclusions based on our audit objectives. We believe that the evidence obtained provides a reasonable basis for our findings and conclusions based on our audit objectives.

In summary, we made the following major points in our original briefing in November 2009:

- The White House and federal agencies have established interagency groups to plan and coordinate CNCI activities. These include the National Cyber Study Group, the Communications Security and Cyber Policy Coordinating Committee, and the Joint Interagency Cyber Task Force. The groups have used status meetings and other reporting mechanisms to track implementation progress of CNCI projects.

- CNCI faces challenges in achieving its objectives related to securing federal information, which include reducing potential vulnerabilities, protecting against intrusion attempts, and anticipating future threats. These challenges include:

  - **Better defining agency roles and responsibilities.** Currently, agencies have overlapping and uncoordinated responsibilities for cybersecurity activities that have not been clarified by the initiative.

  - **Establishing measures of effectiveness.** Measures of the effectiveness of CNCI projects in increasing the cybersecurity of federal information systems have not been developed.

  - **Establishing an appropriate level of transparency.** Current classification of CNCI-related information may hinder the effectiveness of the initiative, particularly with respect to coordinating activities with the private sector and ensuring accountability to the public.

  - **Coordinating interactions with international entities.** None of the projects directly address the coordination of federal cybersecurity activities with international partners.

- **Strategically addressing identity management and authentication.** Homeland Security Presidential Directive 12 (HSPD-12) required a governmentwide standard for secure and reliable forms of identification. However, CNCI does not include any projects focused on enhancing identity authentication (i.e., the identification of people or systems attempting to access federal systems).

- **Reaching agreement on the scope of education efforts.** Stakeholders have not yet reached agreement on the scope of cybersecurity education efforts.

As documented in the briefing, we obtained comments from OMB officials on a draft of the briefing itself, and, among other things, these officials raised concerns that not all of the challenges we identified were associated with specific CNCI projects. In subsequent discussions, these officials reiterated their concern that several of the challenges we identified involved matters that were beyond the scope of the CNCI's 12 projects. In response, we have clarified that two of the challenges we identified—coordinating actions with international entities, and strategically addressing identity management and authentication—are not connected to specific CNCI projects but rather relate to additional cybersecurity activities that are essential to securing federal systems, a key overall goal of CNCI.

In addition, OMB officials called our attention to an initial version of a plan for implementing federal identity, credential, and access management that was released in November 2009, when we presented our briefing. The plan, while not yet complete, is aimed at addressing the challenge we identified regarding identity management and authentication, and we have modified our conclusions and recommendation in this area to take into account this effort.

Conclusions

The White House and federal agencies have taken a number of actions to establish and use interagency mechanisms in planning and coordinating CNCI activities, and these groups have used status meetings and other reporting mechanisms to track the implementation progress of CNCI's component projects. Beginning with the work of the National Cyber Study Group in brainstorming and gathering information from multiple federal sources, the management approach for the initiative has emphasized coordination across agencies.

While planning for CNCI has been broadly coordinated, the initiative faces challenges if it is to fully achieve its objectives related to securing federal information systems, which include reducing potential vulnerabilities, protecting against intrusion attempts, and anticipating future threats. Among other things, roles and responsibilities for participating agencies have not always been clearly defined, and measures of effectiveness have not yet been established. These challenges have been highlighted by experts and in other recent reviews of federal cybersecurity strategies. Until they are addressed within CNCI, the initiative risks not fully meeting its objectives. While these issues relate directly to the projects that comprise CNCI, the federal government also faces strategic challenges in areas that are not the subject of existing projects within CNCI but remain key to achieving the initiative's overall goal of securing federal information systems. These challenges include coordination with international entities and the governmentwide implementation of identity management and authentication.

Recommendations for Executive Action

To address challenges that CNCI faces in achieving its objectives related to securing federal information systems, we are recommending that the Director of OMB take the following four actions:

- better define roles and responsibilities of all key CNCI participants, such as the National Cyber Security Center, to ensure that essential governmentwide cybersecurity activities are fully coordinated;
- establish measures to determine the effectiveness of CNCI projects in making federal information systems more secure and track progress against those measures;
- establish an appropriate level of transparency about CNCI by clarifying the rationale for classifying information, ensuring that as much information is made public as is appropriate, and providing justification for withholding information from the public; and
- reach agreement on the scope of CNCI's education projects to ensure that an adequate cadre of skilled personnel is developed to protect federal information systems.

To address strategic challenges in areas that are not the subject of existing projects within CNCI but remain key to achieving the initiative's overall goal of securing federal information systems, we are recommending that the Director of OMB take the following two actions:

- establish a coordinated approach for the federal government in conducting international outreach to address cybersecurity issues strategically; and
- continue development of a strategic approach to identity management and authentication, linked to HSPD-12 implementation, as initially described in the Chief Information Officers Council's plan for implementing federal identity, credential, and access management, so as to provide greater assurance that only authorized individuals and entities can gain access to federal information systems.

Agency Comments and Our Evaluation

In written comments on a draft of this report, reproduced in appendix II, the Federal Chief Information Officer concurred with five of six recommendations, stating that efforts were either planned or underway to address them. OMB disagreed with our conclusions and recommendation regarding the need to better define roles and responsibilities of federal entities in securing federal systems, noting that specific agency roles and responsibilities for the CNCI initiatives had been clearly defined. We agree that, as described in our briefing, lead responsibility has been assigned for each of the CNCI initiatives. However, this fact does not diminish the larger challenge that CNCI faces in better establishing cybersecurity roles and responsibilities for securing federal systems. For example, as discussed in the briefing, the federal government's response to the July 2009 attacks on its Web sites was not well-coordinated. Although OMB stated that such a response was not an activity specifically within CNCI, the poorly-coordinated response illustrates the larger challenge that CNCI faces in better establishing cybersecurity roles and responsibilities for securing federal systems.

Regarding the statement in the briefing that the National Cyber Security Center (NCSC) has not been fully operational and has had unclear responsibilities, OMB commented that NCSC's responsibilities were distinct from those of other federal entities involved in incident detection and response. However, we disagree. For example, as discussed in the briefing, the United States Computer Emergency Readiness Team (US-CERT), which handles incident response, engages in extensive cross-agency coordination, and it remains unclear how this function differs from the responsibilities planned for NCSC. OMB also stated that it had requested that we clarify that the interagency policy committee is a formal mechanism for interagency coordination. In response to this comment, we previously changed wording in the draft briefing that had incorrectly implied that this committee was an informal mechanism.

The Director of Legislative Affairs of ODNI provided written comments on a draft of this report, which are reproduced in appendix III. In its comments, ODNI expressed concern that comments previously provided on the briefing slides remained largely unincorporated and requested that the report better reflect those comments. Specifically, in its earlier comments, ODNI had raised concern that CNCI should not be criticized for items that were not included in it. As previously discussed, to avoid potential misunderstanding, we have clarified that two of the challenges we identified are not connected to specific CNCI projects but rather relate to additional cybersecurity activities that are necessary to achieve CNCI's overall goal of securing federal information systems.

We are sending copies of this report to the Director of National Intelligence, the Director of the Office of Management and Budget, and to interested congressional committees. The report will also be available on the GAO Web site at no charge at http://www.gao.gov.

If you or your staff have any questions concerning this report, please contact Gregory C. Wilshusen at (202) 512-6244 or wilshuseng@gao.gov, or Davi M. D'Agostino at (202) 512-5431 or dagostinod@gao.gov. Contact points for our Office of Congressional Relations and our Office of Public Affairs may be found on the last page of this report. GAO staff who made major contributions to this report are listed in appendix IV.

Gregory C. Wilshusen
Director, Information Security Issues

Davi M. D'Agostino
Director, Defense Capabilities and Management

Appendix I: Briefing to Congressional Staff on the Comprehensive National Cybersecurity Initiative

INFORMATION SECURITY:
Progress and Challenges in Defining and Coordinating the Comprehensive National Cybersecurity Initiative

Briefing for Staff of the Subcommittee on Terrorism, Unconventional Threats and Capabilities, House Armed Services Committee

November 24, 2009

1

Contents

2

Introduction

Pervasive and sustained cyber attacks against the United States continue to pose the threat of a potentially devastating impact on federal systems and operations. In February 2009, the Director of National Intelligence testified that foreign nations and criminals had targeted government and private sector networks to gain a competitive advantage and potentially disrupt or destroy them, and that terrorist groups had expressed a desire to use cyber attacks as a means to target the United States. As recently as July 2009, press accounts reported that a widespread and coordinated attack over the course of several days targeted Web sites operated by major government agencies, including the Departments of Homeland Security and Defense, the Federal Aviation Administration, and the Federal Trade Commission, causing disruptions to the public availability of government information. Such attacks highlight the importance of developing a concerted response to safeguard federal systems.

In January 2008, President Bush issued National Security Presidential Directive 54/Homeland Security Presidential Directive 23 (NSPD-54/HSPD-23), establishing the Comprehensive National Cybersecurity Initiative (CNCI), a set of projects with the objective of safeguarding federal executive branch government information systems by reducing potential vulnerabilities, protecting against intrusion attempts, and anticipating future threats.

In February 2009, President Obama directed the National Security and Homeland Security Advisors to conduct a review of the plans, programs, and activities underway throughout the government dedicated to cybersecurity, including the CNCI projects. The review resulted in a May 2009 report that recommended areas of action to help achieve a more reliable, resilient, and trustworthy digital infrastructure for the future.

3

Objectives, Scope, and Methodology

Our objectives were to determine

(1) what actions have been taken to develop interagency mechanisms to plan and coordinate CNCI activities, and

(2) what challenges CNCI faces in achieving its objectives related to securing federal information systems.

To determine what actions have been taken to develop interagency mechanisms to plan and coordinate CNCI activities, we analyzed CNCI plans and related agency documentation and interviewed responsible officials at the Office of Management and Budget (OMB), the Department of Homeland Security (DHS), the Office of the Director of National Intelligence (ODNI), the Department of Justice, the Office of Science and Technology Policy (OSTP), the Department of State, and the National Science Foundation. Based on these sources, we compiled a chronology of actions taken related to the planning and coordination of CNCI.

To determine what challenges CNCI faces in achieving its objectives related to securing federal information systems, we identified and reviewed recent studies, including GAO reports, that examined federal cybersecurity issues at the same strategic level addressed by CNCI. We analyzed these studies to identify challenges directly applying to CNCI activities or relevant to the scope of CNCI and compared these with CNCI documentation and reported activities. We interviewed agency officials and recognized cybersecurity experts to confirm the identified challenges and obtain additional information.

4

Objectives, Scope, and Methodology

Our review did not include an assessment of the implementation of the Federal Information Security Management Act,[1] which provides a broad risk-based framework for managing federal information security activities.

We conducted this performance audit from December 2008 to November 2009 in accordance with generally accepted government auditing standards. Those standards require that we plan and perform the audit to obtain sufficient, appropriate evidence to provide a reasonable basis for our findings and conclusions based on our audit objectives. We believe that the evidence obtained provides a reasonable basis for our findings and conclusions based on our audit objectives.

[1]Title III, E-Government Act of 2002, Pub. L. No. 107-347 (Dec. 17, 2002).

5

Results in Brief

Interagency Working Groups Were Established to Plan and Coordinate CNCI Activities

The White House and federal agencies have established interagency groups to plan and coordinate CNCI activities. These groups have used a combination of status meetings and other reporting mechanisms to track implementation progress of CNCI's component projects. For example, agencies have been required to submit reports on progress and issues to an interagency task force, which has compiled the information into quarterly reports provided to the White House and OMB for use in monitoring the progress made by each of the CNCI projects.

6

Results in Brief

CNCI Faces Challenges in Achieving Its Objectives Related to Securing Federal Information Systems

CNCI faces a number of key challenges in achieving its objectives related to securing federal information systems, which include reducing potential vulnerabilities, protecting against intrusion attempts, and anticipating future threats. These challenges include:

- *better defining agency roles and responsibilities*: Currently, agencies have overlapping and uncoordinated responsibilities for cybersecurity activities that have not been clarified in CNCI. CNCI is unlikely to achieve its goals until these roles are better clarified.
- *establishing measures of effectiveness*: Measures of the effectiveness of CNCI activities in increasing the cybersecurity of federal information systems have not yet been developed. Without such measures, the extent to which CNCI is achieving its goal of reducing potential vulnerabilities, protecting against intrusion attempts, and anticipating future threats is unclear.
- *balancing transparency with classification requirements*: Few elements of CNCI have been made public, and the rationale for how agencies classify information related to CNCI activities remains unclear. The lack of transparency regarding CNCI projects hinders accountability to Congress and the public. In addition, current classification may make it difficult for some agencies, as well as the private sector, to interact and contribute to the success of CNCI projects.

7

Results in Brief

- *coordinating interactions with international partners*: None of the 12 projects comprising CNCI directly address the coordination of international activities, which includes facilitating cooperation between cybersecurity and law enforcement professionals in different nations, developing security standards, and pursuing international agreements on engagement and information sharing. By addressing these issues in a coordinated way, CNCI could better achieve its objectives related to securing federal information systems.
- *strategically addressing identity management and authentication*: The federal government has long been challenged in employing effective identity management and authentication technologies; however, CNCI does not include an effort strategically focused on enhancing identity authentication across the federal government. CNCI is unlikely to be fully successful without addressing identity management and authentication.
- *reaching agreement on the scope of education efforts*: CNCI stakeholders have not yet reached agreement on whether the initiative should focus strictly on training the current workforce or include K-12, college, and graduate-level programs. Until agreement is reached, cybersecurity education will not be fully addressed by CNCI.

We are recommending that the Director of National Intelligence and the Director of the Office of Management and Budget take steps to address these challenges within CNCI.

8

Results in Brief

We provided a draft of this briefing to OMB, ODNI, and the Department of State for review and comment. In comments provided via e-mail, OMB stated that it agreed that many areas of federal cybersecurity could use improvement but disagreed that these issues are all related to CNCI. Similarly, ODNI agreed that the challenges we identified should have been included or accounted for in CNCI but raised concern that the program should not be criticized for items that were not included in it. We agree that CNCI was not intended to subsume all activities related to cybersecurity and have clarified our briefing to avoid a potential misunderstanding. Nevertheless, we believe that the challenges we identified remain of critical importance in determining whether CNCI can achieve its objectives related to securing federal information systems. The State Department did not indicate whether it agreed or disagreed with the content of the briefing. OMB, ODNI, and State also provided technical comments that we have addressed as appropriate in the final briefing.

9

Background

In January 2008, the President issued National Security Presidential Directive 54/Homeland Security Presidential Directive 23 (NSPD-54/HSPD-23), establishing the Comprehensive National Cybersecurity Initiative (CNCI), a set of projects designed to safeguard federal government information systems by reducing potential vulnerabilities, protecting against intrusion attempts, and anticipating future threats.

According to the Department of Homeland Security (DHS), the three overall goals of CNCI are to

- establish a frontline defense—reduce current vulnerabilities and prevent intrusions;
- defend against the full spectrum of threats by using intelligence and strengthening supply chain security; and
- shape the future environment by enhancing research, development, and education as well as investing in leap-ahead technologies.

10

Background

NSPD-54/HSPD-23 established 12 CNCI projects and identified lead agencies for each.[2] Since January 2008, the lead agencies have been responsible for tracking progress on each of the projects specified in the directive.

Four agencies have responsibilities for multiple projects of CNCI:

- DHS's responsibilities focus on protecting civilian agency information systems, including reducing and consolidating external access points, deploying passive network sensors, and defining public and private partnerships.
- The Department of Defense (DOD) is charged with monitoring military information systems, increasing the security of classified networks, and deploying intrusion prevention systems, among other things.
- ODNI is responsible for monitoring intelligence community information systems and other intelligence-related activities, including the development of a governmentwide cyber counterintelligence plan.
- OSTP, which is responsible for providing advice on the effects of science and technology on domestic and international affairs, is responsible for the two CNCI projects that focus on advanced technology research and development.

OMB, the Department of Justice, and the National Security Council also have lead roles on specific CNCI projects.

[2]With the exception of DHS, budget data for CNCI projects is classified. In fiscal year 2009, $254.9 million was appropriated for DHS activities related to CNCI efforts. According to DHS officials, the President's fiscal year 2010 budget proposed $334 million to support CNCI at DHS.

11

Background

Table 1 lists and describes all 12 projects, and identifies the lead agency or agencies responsible for each.

Table 1: CNCI Projects and Lead Agencies

Project	Description	Lead agency/agencies
Trusted Internet Connections	Reduce and consolidate external access points with the goal of limiting points of access to the Internet for executive branch civilian agencies	OMB / DHS
Einstein 2	Deploy passive sensors across executive branch civilian systems that have the ability to scan the content of Internet packets to determine whether they contain malicious code	DHS
Einstein 3	Pursue deployment of intrusion prevention system that will allow for real-time prevention capabilities that will assess and block harmful code	DHS / DOD
Research and Development Efforts	Coordinate and redirect research and development (R&D) efforts with a focus on coordinating both classified and unclassified R&D for cybersecurity	OSTP
Connecting the Centers (includes National Cyber Security Center)	Connect current cyber centers to enhance cyber situational awareness and lead to greater integration and understanding of the cyber threat	ODNI

12

Background

Project	Description	Lead agency/agencies
Cyber Counterintelligence Plan	Develop governmentwide cyber counterintelligence plan by improving the security of the physical and electromagnetic integrity of U.S. networks	ODNI / Department of Justice
Security of Classified Networks	Increase the security of classified networks to reduce the risk of information contained on the government's classified networks being disclosed	DOD / ODNI
Expand Education	Expand education efforts by constructing a comprehensive federal cyber education and training program, with attention to offensive and defensive skills and capabilities	DHS / DOD
Leap-Ahead Technology	Define and develop enduring leap-ahead technology, strategies, and programs by investing in high-risk, high-reward research and development and by working with both private sector and international partners	OSTP
Deterrence Strategies and Programs	Define and develop enduring deterrence strategies and programs that focus on reducing vulnerabilities and deter interference and attack in cyberspace	National Security Council
Global Supply Chain Risk Management	Develop multi-pronged approach for global supply chain risk management while seeking to better manage the federal government's global supply chain	DHS / DOD
Public and Private Partnerships "Project 12"	Define the federal role for extending cyber security into critical infrastructure domains and seek to define new mechanisms for the federal government and industry to work together to protect the nation's critical infrastructure	DHS

Source: GAO analysis of DHS and publicly available information.

13

Background

Several studies and expert groups have presented findings and recommendations that relate to the progress and comprehensiveness of CNCI. For example, in December 2008, the Center for Strategic and International Studies (CSIS), a bipartisan, nonprofit research and analysis organization, released a report by its Commission on Cybersecurity for the 44th Presidency which noted that although the CNCI was a good start, it was not sufficient to address the urgent national security problem of protecting cyberspace. The report concluded that the new administration should adopt the efforts of CNCI and work toward a comprehensive approach to cybersecurity.

Similarly, in March 2009 we reported on panel discussions we held with experts on critical aspects of the nation's cybersecurity strategy, including areas for improvement.[3] The experts, who included former federal officials, academics, and private sector executives, highlighted key improvements that were, in their view, essential to updating the strategy and our national cybersecurity posture. Improvements they identified include developing a national strategy that clearly articulates strategic objectives, goals, and priorities and establishing a governance structure for implementing the strategy.

[3]GAO, *National Cybersecurity Strategy: Key Improvements Are Needed to Strengthen the Nation's Posture*, GAO-09-432T (Washington, D.C.: March 10, 2009).

14

Background

In May 2009, the President announced the results of a policy review of the plans, programs, and activities underway throughout the government dedicated to cybersecurity, including CNCI. The report recommended that CNCI activities be evaluated as one near-term action to help achieve a more reliable, resilient, and trustworthy digital infrastructure for the future.

As the policy review recommended, the President established a cybersecurity coordinator position to, among other things, integrate the government's cybersecurity policies. The policy review recommended that the coordinator perform the following actions related to CNCI:

- **Revise the nation's cyber strategy.** The review recommended that the cybersecurity coordinator prepare an updated national strategy to secure the information and communications infrastructure, including a continued evaluation of CNCI activities. The review recommended that consideration be given to the need for adjustments or additions to CNCI implementation plans.

- **Consider options for monitoring and coordination responsibilities.** The review noted that various oversight functions for cybersecurity efforts were performed outside of the Executive Office of the President. During the course of the review, a variety of structural options were suggested for the cybersecurity coordinator to coordinate and oversee cybersecurity activities, several of which would establish oversight responsibilities for CNCI within OMB or the Executive Office of the President.

These actions have not yet been implemented.

15

Interagency Coordination Mechanisms
National Cyber Study Group

Interagency Working Groups Were Established to Plan and Coordinate CNCI Activities

The White House and key agencies took several actions to develop interagency mechanisms to plan and coordinate the proposed projects that would be grouped together as the CNCI. Existing interagency working groups were used and new ones established to develop and coordinate the planned projects. Specific groups used or established in connection with development of CNCI included:

- **National Cyber Study Group (NCSG).** The NCSG was the original interagency group that was convened to do brainstorming and information-gathering as preparation for establishment of CNCI, according to key agency officials involved in the group. In May 2007, the President directed the Director of National Intelligence to conduct a review of the federal government's cybersecurity status. In response, the Director established the NCSG, composed of senior executives from over 20 agencies, led by ODNI. During the course of its work, the NCSG gathered information about major civilian, defense, and intelligence agencies to understand their roles and responsibilities in federal cybersecurity efforts. The NCSG met twice a week for several months to understand agencies' roles in national cybersecurity, their capabilities, and the overall threats to federal networks.

16

Interagency Coordination Mechanisms
Policy Coordinating Committee

- **Communications Security and Cyber Policy Coordinating Committee (PCC).** The PCC, a White House coordinating committee, was the chief mechanism used for presenting final CNCI plans to the President and coordinating initial implementation actions after the program was approved, according to key agency officials involved with the group.[4] In late 2007, the NCSG transferred its initial planning work on CNCI to the PCC, which was co-chaired by the Homeland Security Council (HSC) and the National Security Council (NSC), and had been in existence prior to taking on the CNCI task. Six sub-groups of the PCC were established as focal points for specific issues to support the work of the larger committee.

Shortly after the transfer from NCSG, the PCC presented its CNCI proposal to the President. The proposal included a set of cybersecurity projects that would make up the initiative. The White House used this as the basis for NSPD-54/HSPD-23, which was approved by the President in January 2008.

The PCC immediately began overseeing CNCI implementation. According to an OMB official, in the 12 months following the approval of NSPD-54/HSPD-23, the PCC met weekly to assess CNCI projects' performance. Once a quarter, a meeting was held to conduct a more in-depth review of the projects.

[4]Following the change in administration in 2009, the PCC was re-named the Information and Communications Infrastructure Interagency Policy Committee (ICI IPC).

17

Interagency Coordination Mechanisms
Joint Interagency Cyber Task Force

- **Joint Interagency Cyber Task Force.** According to ODNI, NSPD-54/HSPD-23 assigned it the responsibility to monitor and coordinate the implementation of CNCI, and to do so in coordination with the Secretaries of State, the Treasury, Defense, Commerce, Energy, and Homeland Security, and the Attorney General.

To address these responsibilities, ODNI established a Joint Interagency Cyber Task Force (JIACTF) in February 2008. The mission of the task force was to serve as the focal point for monitoring and coordinating the CNCI projects and to enable the participation of both Intelligence Community (IC) and non-IC agencies in the overall CNCI effort. Its responsibilities included establishing performance measures for monitoring implementation of the initiative.

According to the acting director of the JIACTF, although ODNI served as a coordinator through the task force, it was not authorized to direct other agencies to complete CNCI tasks. The acting director stated that ODNI is only responsible for monitoring and reporting to the President on CNCI activities.

18

Interagency Coordination Mechanisms
Interagency Working Groups

The JIACTF and PCC used a combination of status meetings and other reporting mechanisms to track implementation progress of the CNCI's component projects:

- **Interagency Working Groups.** For each of the CNCI projects, interagency working groups developed specific deliverables called for by the presidential directive, such as implementation plans and other reports.

According to ODNI, the JIACTF assisted each working group in drafting 3-, 9-, 18-, and 36-month target implementation goals, against which their progress was to be measured by the JIACTF.[5] According to ODNI, the measures were established to ensure that CNCI deliverables were being submitted in a timely manner and that the White House was aware of when actions were due or of unresolved issues. ODNI reported that over 80 measures were being tracked.

[5]ODNI noted that implementation goals were also included for 12-, 24-, and 30-month activities for some initiatives.

19

Interagency Coordination Mechanisms

Quarterly Reports

- **Quarterly Reports.** Agencies were required to submit reports on progress and issues to the JIACTF, which compiled aggregate reports based on these submissions. According to ODNI, the task force conducted follow-up meetings with agency leads to address any outstanding issues. In addition, it met quarterly with CNCI project leads to conduct in-depth discussions of successes, remaining challenges, and risks.

On a quarterly basis, the task force submitted reports to the White House, with copies provided to OMB, outlining the status of CNCI and offering recommendations. The reports indicated which activities were on schedule or needed further attention by JIACTF members. According to ODNI, these reports reflected discussions with agency leads and focused on target achievements, recent accomplishments, planned activities and schedules, challenges, risks and mitigation strategies, information on budget and staffing, performance measures, critical issues, and recommendations. An OMB official stated that the content of these reports became more detailed over time.

20

Interagency Coordination Mechanisms

The following figure summarizes key actions to develop interagency mechanisms for coordinating CNCI in the context of other related cybersecurity events.

Figure 1: Timeline of Actions to Develop Interagency Mechanisms and Other CNCI-Related Events

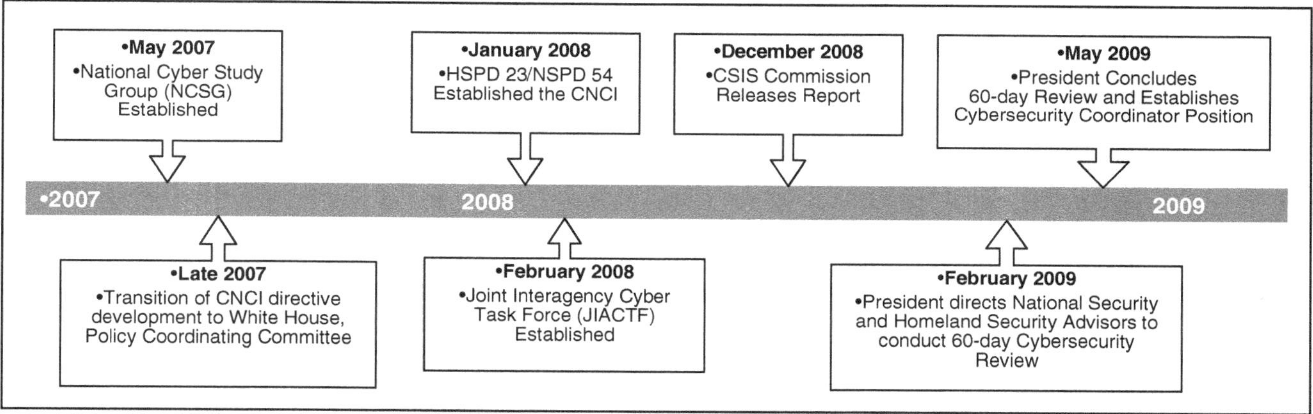

Source: GAO analysis of agency data.

21

CNCI Faces Challenges
Roles and Responsibilities

CNCI Faces Challenges in Achieving its Objectives Related to Securing Federal Information Systems

CNCI faces a number of key challenges in achieving its objectives related to securing federal information systems, which include reducing potential vulnerabilities, protecting against intrusion attempts, and anticipating future threats.

Better Defining Agency Roles and Responsibilities

We previously reported that clearly defining areas of responsibility is a key internal control that provides management with a framework for planning, directing, and controlling operations to achieve goals.[6] To collaborate effectively, agencies need to define and agree on their respective roles and responsibilities, including how the collaborative effort will be led. Doing so can help to organize joint and individual efforts and facilitate decision-making.[7] Commitment by those involved in the collaborative effort, from all levels of the organization, is also critical to overcoming the many barriers to working across agency boundaries. Clearly defining roles and responsibilities in securing federal information systems is particularly important because such systems are highly interconnected, and their security is a critical element of the nation's overall security.

[6]GAO, *Internal Control: Standards for Internal Control in the Federal Government*, GAO/AIMD-00-21.3.1 (Washington, D.C.: November 1999).

[7]GAO, *Results-Oriented Government: Practices That Can Help Enhance and Sustain Collaboration among Federal Agencies*, GAO-06-15 (Washington, D.C.: October 21, 2005).

22

CNCI Faces Challenges
Roles and Responsibilities

Currently, agencies have overlapping and uncoordinated responsibilities for cybersecurity activities that have not been clarified by CNCI. A key example is the lack of agreement regarding which agency is responsible for leading efforts in cyber information sharing and situational awareness. Specifically, NSPD-54/HSPD-23 directed the Secretary of Homeland Security to establish a National Cyber Security Center (NCSC) to coordinate and integrate information to secure networks and systems. However, several other cybersecurity response centers—including one within DHS—have many of the same responsibilities as NCSC for coordinating the federal response to cybersecurity incidents. According to the then-acting director of the NCSC, due to a lack of coordination among the top level of agencies and the White House, the center has not been fully operational, and it was unclear what responsibilities it was to assume for the federal government as a whole.

Further, the Secretary of Homeland Security recently stated that DHS was not sufficiently organized to achieve the goals of interagency cybersecurity programs, which include CNCI projects at DHS. The Secretary stated that all cyber responsibilities at DHS were moved under the Deputy Under Secretary for National Protection and Programs in June to address this issue. However, the acting director of the NCSC noted that the NCSC remains separate from other DHS cybersecurity programs and is still not fully operational. Specifically, she stated that although the NCSC is now funded through the National Protection and Programs Directorate, it continues to report independently to the Secretary of Homeland Security.

23

CNCI Faces Challenges
Roles and Responsibilities

Another example of overlapping and uncoordinated responsibilities is federal agencies' response to the July 2009 cyber attacks on U.S. government Web sites. The Acting White House Cybersecurity Policy Advisor noted that agencies had responded in an ad hoc manner to these attacks and that the response had not been well-coordinated. She added that to establish specific roles, functions, and relationships among federal government security personnel in responding to an incident, DHS plans to develop a national incident response plan by the end of 2009.

While not addressing the specifics of CNCI project roles and responsibilities, experts have discussed the broader challenge of overlapping roles and responsibilities regarding federal cybersecurity, which has an impact on achieving CNCI objectives. For example:

- The CSIS commission stated that the central problems in the current federal organization for cybersecurity are lack of a strategic focus, overlapping missions, poor coordination and collaboration, and diffuse responsibility. To combat these challenges, the commission recommended the creation of a new cyberspace office in the Executive Office of the President that could leverage the knowledge of resources across federal agencies in order to provide the best security for our nation.
- Our expert panel raised concerns about how national security agencies coordinate with law enforcement agencies on issues of cybersecurity. Specifically, they stated that national security agencies often times overlooked the value and resources that law enforcement agencies had to offer on cybersecurity issues.

24

CNCI Faces Challenges
Roles and Responsibilities

- The White House policy review stated that the federal government is not organized to effectively address cybersecurity challenges. Specifically, it stated that responsibilities for cybersecurity are distributed across a wide array of federal agencies, many with overlapping authorities, and none with sufficient decision authority to direct actions that allow for consistency in dealing with often-conflicting issues. The policy review recommended that the President's new cybersecurity policy official work with agencies to recommend coherent, unified policy guidance where necessary to clarify authorities, roles, and responsibilities for cybersecurity-related activities across the federal government.

CNCI is unlikely to fully achieve its goal of reducing potential vulnerabilities, protecting against intrusion attempts, and anticipating future threats to federal information systems unless roles and responsibilities for cybersecurity activities across the federal government are more clearly defined and coordinated.

25

CNCI Faces Challenges
Effectiveness Metrics

Establishing Measures of Effectiveness

As we previously reported, measuring performance allows organizations to track the progress they are making toward their goals and gives managers crucial information on which to base their organizational and management decisions.[8] For example, performance metrics are valuable to management when forecasting future budgetary needs. Leading organizations also recognize that performance measures can create powerful incentives to influence organizational and individual behavior. Additionally, when appropriate, making performance measurements available to the public demonstrates transparency, allowing the public to see evidence of program effectiveness.

Measures of the effectiveness of CNCI activities in increasing the cybersecurity of federal information systems have not yet been developed. Although CNCI plans contain milestones for tracking implementation progress (such as the timely submission of development deliverables), they do not have corresponding benchmarks for effectiveness to gauge the extent to which CNCI activities are improving cybersecurity.

[8]GAO, *Executive Guide: Effectively Implementing the Government Performance and Results Act,* GAO/GGD-96-118 (Washington, D.C.: June 1996).

26

CNCI Faces Challenges
Effectiveness Metrics

While two of the CNCI implementation plans we reviewed outlined future efforts to establish performance measures to assess progress towards achieving the initiatives' goals, other plans did not include such measures. Specifically, the Research and Development Coordination and Leap-Ahead Technologies initiatives planned to set measures for, among other things, quality of research, direct impact (where research results are adopted for operational use), and indirect impact (such as developing new collaborations or technology transfer agreements). Other CNCI projects had not defined measures such as these. OMB stated that it intends to develop effectiveness metrics once the implementation stages of the projects are finished.

The federal government has recently begun taking action to develop effectiveness metrics for information security, and the results of these efforts may be applicable to CNCI. For example, recently, the federal CIO Council—the principal interagency forum for federal chief information officers—began efforts to promote the development and use of standard performance metrics that measure improvements in agencies' security posture over time and ensure that collaborative federal cybersecurity capabilities are prioritized. In addition, OMB has begun assembling a working group of federal agencies, advisory groups, and private sector partners to develop information security metrics that give insight into agencies' security postures on an on-going basis. OMB plans to release its new metrics by February 2010. While these efforts could assist CNCI implementation by developing effectiveness measures for use across the federal government, neither is currently part of CNCI.

27

CNCI Faces Challenges
Effectiveness Metrics

The importance of measuring the effectiveness of cybersecurity programs has been underscored in recent assessments:

- The CSIS commission stated that a central part of judging whether a product or initiative has improved security is to develop metrics that can measure progress. However, the commission added that the federal government lacks meaningful measures of security. In addition, the commission stated that agencies should place greater emphasis on the periodic testing of information security procedures, policies, and practices required by the Federal Information Security Management Act of 2002 (FISMA). It added that agencies could use "red-team" attack assessments and recorded outcomes, in addition to the FISMA testing, as inputs to their effectiveness metrics.[9]
- The recent White House policy review stated the need for cybersecurity programs to have a defined purpose and metrics to evaluate whether their goals are achieved. Specifically, within its near-time action plan, it recommended designating cybersecurity as one of the President's key management priorities and establishing performance metrics.

[9]"Red team" simulated network attack exercises are used as a way to test responsiveness and evaluate different aspects of an agency's overall security posture. Recorded outcomes of activities as a result of the simulation—such as the amount of time it takes for a password, network, or server to be compromised—can be used by management to prioritize projects aimed at reducing cyber attack risks.

28

CNCI Faces Challenges
Effectiveness Metrics

- In September 2009, we reported on the current shortcomings of performance metrics for evaluating federal agencies' information security controls and programs.[10] Specifically, we reported that federal agencies had tended to rely on measures of compliance with legal requirements, internal policies, or industry standards. We noted that until OMB revises its reporting guidance to require a more balanced range of measures and adherence to key practices in developing those measures, agencies are likely to continue to predominantly rely on measures that are of only limited value in assessing the effectiveness of their information security programs.

Without mechanisms to measure the effectiveness of federal cybersecurity efforts, the extent to which CNCI is achieving its goal of reducing potential vulnerabilities, protecting against intrusion attempts, and anticipating future threats is unclear. Particularly for agencies with multiple cyber responsibilities, both inside and outside of CNCI, effectiveness metrics would assist with prioritizing projects to get the best results. Establishing such measures would, as appropriate, allow federal officials, Congress, and the public to determine how effective CNCI projects and other cybersecurity efforts are at making federal information systems more secure.

[10]GAO, *Information Security: Concerted Effort Needed to Improve Federal Performance Measures*, GAO-09-617 (Washington, D.C.: September 14, 2009).

29

CNCI Faces Challenges
Transparency

Establishing an Appropriate Level of Transparency

We previously reported that transparency is essential to improving government performance, ensuring accountability, and maintaining public trust. An appropriate level of transparency requires finding the right balance between restricting access to sensitive information and making such information available to Congress, other government agencies, private sector and international partners, and the public.[11] In January 2009, the President issued a memorandum to the heads of executive departments and agencies, committing them to greater transparency to promote accountability and provide information for citizens about what their government is doing.

Since the approval of NSPD-54/HSPD-23, few elements of CNCI have been made public. For example, agency press releases and statements by government officials have provided limited information regarding CNCI and its component projects. In addition, while OMB released guidance on the implementation of the governmentwide Trusted Internet Connections project, which aims to reduce connection points between agencies and the Internet, few details have been publicly released for other projects, such as Einstein 3 and Deterrence Strategies and Programs. The Einstein 3 project, which aims to prevent intrusion into federal networks by scrutinizing Internet traffic, has raised privacy concerns, but DHS has yet to release documentation of Einstein 3's privacy protection mechanisms.

[11]GAO, *Transparent Government and Access to Information: A Role for Supreme Audit Institutions,* GAO-07-1068CG (Washington, D.C.: June 26, 2007).

30

CNCI Faces Challenges
Transparency

Further, NSPD-54/HSPD-23 itself was written at a classified level and remains so. Officials from the Department of State and the National Cyber Security Center stated that the classification level of the directive hindered their ability to work with outside organizations. They added that the JIACTF and White House are planning to review the directive and CNCI projects to determine whether portions should be declassified.

The rationale for how agencies classify information related to CNCI activities remains unclear. For example, the supply chain risk management program presumably engages the private sector, but is entirely classified at the Secret level and higher. While DHS officials stated that a CNCI classification guide had been developed by ODNI, they did not provide a copy. DHS officials were also unable to provide justification for decisions made about which aspects of the initiative to make public.

Since CNCI's inception, former and current government officials have voiced concerns regarding the lack of publicly available information. For example:

- The federally-chartered Information Security and Privacy Advisory Board (ISPAB) stated that greater clarity and transparency was necessary to ensure both the effectiveness and trustworthiness of CNCI. Specifically, the ISPAB advised that government agencies release key documentation regarding the impact of CNCI activities on personal privacy.

31

CNCI Faces Challenges
Transparency

- The CSIS commission noted that because the CNCI directive and projects are classified, little information could be shared with the public, the cybersecurity industry, or allied nations. The commission concluded that greater openness is important given the large role played by those outside the federal government in cybersecurity. In addition, the commission stated that the United States should open the discussion of how best to secure cyberspace and present the issues of deterrence and national strategy to the broad national community of experts and stakeholders.
- The White House policy review stated that, in moving forward, transparency would be important to build trust between the public and federal cybersecurity programs. The review added that it would be important to bring transparency and effective management to the overall cybersecurity portfolio.

While certain aspects and details of CNCI must necessarily remain classified, the lack of transparency regarding CNCI projects hinders accountability to Congress and the public. In addition, current classification may make it difficult for some agencies, as well as the private sector, to interact and contribute to the success of CNCI projects.

32

CNCI Faces Challenges
International Outreach

Coordinating Interactions with International Entities

Federal information systems operate in a cyberspace that is affected by individuals and nations from all over the world. Effective federal cybersecurity requires coordinated interaction with other nations. For example:

- *Pursuing law enforcement investigations and prosecutions* – Criminals operating in cyberspace can route their attacks through multiple computers located in different nations. As law enforcement officials trace such illegal activities across national boundaries, they must work with officials from those nations for permission and assistance in continuing the investigations. According to FBI officials, in order to pursue investigations quickly and efficiently, cybersecurity and law enforcement professionals must have agreements in place that facilitate cooperation.
- *Developing security standards for the Internet* – Communications and transactions in cyberspace occur over a common, global infrastructure (the Internet). Federal information systems connect to the Internet to communicate with contractor systems, the public, and other agency systems. Major decisions regarding the technical aspects of the Internet, such as security elements within common protocols and management of the Internet are increasingly being debated at an international level. The Acting White House Cybersecurity Policy Advisor has stated that to ensure that federal requirements are taken into account in these discussions, the federal government needs to carefully coordinate its participation.

33

CNCI Faces Challenges
International Outreach

- *Defining rules of engagement* – The severity of recent cyber incidents has raised questions about the types of actions government agencies may take to defend themselves from attack. For example, agency officials may wish to disable a computer attacking from another nation in order to stop the attack. Further, acceptable behavior for engaging attackers in cyberspace may evolve as new technologies and types of attacks are created. In this regard, as the CSIS commission has pointed out, establishing a coordinated process for proposing and refining rules of engagement and negotiating related agreements with foreign governments is of critical importance.
- *Sharing information for situational awareness* – Exchanging information about recent attacks with other nations is critical for cybersecurity professionals to understand vulnerabilities, attack methods, and other current and emerging trends. According to the White House policy review, it is also necessary for coordinating responses to international cyber incidents.

The coordination of federal cybersecurity activities with international entities was not included within the scope of CNCI. Various agencies have independent efforts underway to address international cybersecurity issues. However, none of the 12 CNCI projects directly address the coordination of international activities.

34

CNCI Faces Challenges
International Outreach

The federal government has not fully resolved issues regarding how to coordinate international cybersecurity activities. For example, according to FBI officials, federal agencies have relied on relationships that they have established individually with international partners to share information regarding law enforcement investigations. The officials stated that a formal interagency mechanism had not yet been developed to coordinate engagement with international partners on such investigations.

According to Department of State and FBI officials, a sub-group of the White House interagency policy committee that oversees CNCI projects acts as a forum for the coordination of international cybersecurity activities. However, the group has not developed a formal strategy for coordinating international outreach.

Experts have also identified international outreach on cybersecurity issues as a major challenge to the federal government. For example:

- The CSIS commission noted that the international aspects of cybersecurity have been among the least developed elements of U.S. cybersecurity policy. The commission added that CNCI is lacking in efforts to coordinate with international partners.
- Our panel of cybersecurity experts stated that greater attention must be focused on addressing the global aspects of cyberspace, including developing treaties, establishing standards, and pursuing international agreements. For example, panel members stated that the U.S. should pursue a more coordinated, aggressive approach.

35

CNCI Faces Challenges
International Outreach

- The White House policy review reiterated the need for a strategy for cybersecurity designed to shape the international environment and bring like-minded nations together on a host of issues, such as technical standards, acceptable legal norms, sovereign responsibility, and the use of force. For example, the policy review pointed out that the Council of Europe Convention on Cybercrime was an important international effort to achieve consistency in cybercrime laws and law enforcement efforts that had yet to be endorsed by many nations.

Addressing international efforts includes improving cooperation between cybersecurity and law enforcement professionals in different nations, developing security standards, and pursuing international agreements on engagement and information sharing. By addressing these issues in a coordinated way, CNCI could better achieve its objectives related to securing federal information systems.

36

CNCI Faces Challenges

Identity Management and Authentication

Strategically Addressing Identity Management and Authentication

Confirming the identity of people and systems attempting to access federal networks is an essential step in ensuring the security of those information systems. As we previously reported, this confirmation process, known as authentication, provides assurance that only authorized individuals and other entities can gain appropriate access to federal information systems. Authentication and identity management use a variety of technologies, including passwords, electronic identification cards, and biometric identifiers, to provide different levels of assurance based on the sensitivity of the data being protected.[12]

The federal government has long been challenged in employing effective identity management and authentication technologies. For example, in an effort to increase the quality and security of federal identification and credentialing practices, the President issued Homeland Security Presidential Directive 12 (HSPD-12) in August 2004, requiring the establishment of a governmentwide standard for secure and reliable forms of identification. However, as we have previously reported, agencies have struggled to implement the authentication requirements of HSPD-12.[13] For example, most agencies had not made full use of the electronic authentication capabilities available on the personal identification verification cards that they had issued or had plans to do so.

[12]GAO, *Electronic Government: Additional OMB Leadership Needed to Optimize Use of New Federal Employee Identification Cards,* GAO-08-292 (Washington, D.C.: February 29, 2008).

[13]GAO-08-292.

37

CNCI Faces Challenges
Identity Management and Authentication

CNCI does not include any projects focused on enhancing identity authentication. Instead, its operational projects are dedicated to areas such as intrusion detection and prevention, limiting the number of Internet nodes, and deterrence strategies. While these are important, there is no strategic effort to address the issue of authenticating users appropriately and consistently across federal systems and networks.

Cybersecurity experts have reaffirmed the need for identity management and authentication across the federal government. For example:

- The National Science and Technology Council—the principal group within the White House to coordinate policy among federal research and development agencies—reported in 2008 on major deficiencies in federal identity management efforts.[14] The council concluded that the federal government is only beginning to work toward a consistent approach to identity management, and that there is no single organization responsible for coordinating governmentwide identity management.

[14]The National Science and Technology Council, *Identity Management Task Force Report 2008* (Washington D.C., 2008).

38

CNCI Faces Challenges
Identity Management and Authentication

- According to the CSIS commission, strong authentication significantly improves defensive capabilities, but the federal government has not succeeded in improving authentication, and it is not addressed by the CNCI directive. The commission recommended that the President require agencies to report on the status of their compliance with HSPD-12 and restrict bonuses and awards at agencies that have not fully complied with the implementation of the directive.
- The White House policy review stated that cybersecurity cannot be improved without improving authentication. Specifically, it stated that the federal government—in collaboration with industry and the civil liberties and privacy communities—should build a cybersecurity-based identity management vision and strategy for the nation that considers an array of approaches, including privacy-enhancing technologies. It further stated that the federal government should ensure resources are available for full federal implementation of HSPD-12. In July 2009, the Acting White House Cybersecurity Policy Advisor stated that work had begun on a framework to set priorities in the area of identity management.

Using strong methods of identifying people and systems attempting to access federal systems and sensitive information is an essential part of a comprehensive security program to strengthen cybersecurity. Without a strategic approach to enhancing identity management and authentication linked to HSPD-12 implementation, CNCI is unlikely to be fully successful in addressing the security of the federal government's information systems and assets.

39

CNCI Faces Challenges
Scope of Education Efforts

Reaching Agreement on the Scope of Education Efforts

Training and education within the federal government are key for ensuring that safe and secure practices are exercised by federal employees when they access government information systems. In addition, our panel of cybersecurity experts stated that the federal government should raise public awareness about the seriousness of cybersecurity issues and that many national leaders in business and government are generally not aware of the severity of the risks to national and economic security posed by cybersecurity threats. Further, in order to maintain the security of federal information systems, agencies need properly trained cybersecurity professionals.

DHS's cybersecurity education efforts currently focus on the training and education of the current and future federal workforce. According to the lead DHS official for cybersecurity education, the CNCI directive requires DHS and DOD to develop a strategy and recommendations for prioritizing and redirecting current educational efforts to build a skilled cyber workforce and ensuring the development of skilled individuals for future federal government employment.

40

CNCI Faces Challenges
Scope of Education Efforts

However, CNCI stakeholders have not yet reached agreement on the scope of CNCI education efforts. According to the DHS official responsible for the CNCI education initiative, an interagency working group tasked with advising the education initiative has discussed the importance of broadening the scope of education efforts to include K-12, college, and graduate-level cybersecurity education. The DHS official responsible for cybersecurity education stated that one example of such efforts was the Centers of Academic Excellence in Information Assurance Education program; in this program, students can take better cybersecurity practices with them into the private sector, which is ultimately better for the federal government as a consumer of private sector goods and services. However, the White House has not yet approved the CNCI education implementation plan. According to the DHS official for cybersecurity education, some administration officials believe the plan should focus strictly on training the current workforce, rather than having a broader scope to include efforts for K-12 education and the college and graduate levels.

Experts have also discussed the challenge of expanding cybersecurity education and the federal cyber workforce. For example:

- The CSIS commission stated that there was neither a broad cadre of cyber experts nor an established cyber career field to build upon. It recommended increasing the supply of skilled workers, possibly through increasing scholarships, and developing a career path for cyber specialists in federal service.

41

CNCI Faces Challenges
Scope of Education Efforts

- According to our expert panel, the federal government needs to publicize and raise awareness of the seriousness of the cybersecurity problem and to increase the number of professionals with adequate cybersecurity skills. Expert panel members stated that the cybersecurity discipline should be organized into concrete professional tracks through testing and licensing. Such tracks would increase the federal cybersecurity workforce by strengthening the hiring and retention of cybersecurity professionals.
- The White House policy review discussed education and workforce development as important parts of the national cybersecurity strategy. In particular, the policy review recommended
  - initiating a national public awareness and education campaign to promote cybersecurity;
  - expanding support for key education programs and research and development to ensure the nation's continued ability to compete in the information age economy; and
  - developing a strategy to expand and train the workforce, including attracting and retaining cybersecurity expertise in the federal government.

42

CNCI Faces Challenges
Scope of Education Efforts

- The Partnership for Public Service, a non-profit policy group, recently released a study finding that the federal government faces major challenges in attracting, hiring, training, retaining, and effectively managing cybersecurity talent.[15] They added that the federal government would be unable to combat cybersecurity threats without a more coordinated, sustained effort to increase cybersecurity expertise in the federal workforce.

Until agency officials agree on the scope of CNCI's education efforts, public awareness and broad cybersecurity education will not be fully addressed by the CNCI.

[15]Partnership for Public Service, *Cyber IN-Security: Strengthening the Federal Cybersecurity Workforce* (Washington D.C., July 2009).

43

Conclusions

The White House and federal agencies have taken a number of actions to establish and use interagency mechanisms in planning and coordinating CNCI activities, and these groups have used status meetings and other reporting mechanisms to track the implementation progress of CNCI's component projects. Beginning with the work of the National Cyber Study Group in brainstorming and gathering information from multiple federal sources, the management approach for the initiative has emphasized coordination across agencies.

While planning for CNCI has been broadly coordinated, the initiative faces challenges if it is to achieve its objectives related to securing federal information systems, which include reducing potential vulnerabilities, protecting against intrusion attempts, and anticipating future threats. Among other things, roles and responsibilities for participating agencies have not always been clearly defined, measures of effectiveness have not yet been established, and key issues—such as coordination with international entities and the governmentwide implementation of identity management and authentication—have not received strategic attention. These challenges have been highlighted by experts and in other recent reviews of federal cybersecurity strategies. Until they are addressed within CNCI, the initiative risks not fully meeting its objectives.

44

Recommendations for Executive Action

We are recommending that the Director of National Intelligence and the Director of the Office of Management and Budget address the challenges that CNCI faces in achieving its objectives related to securing federal information systems by taking the following six actions:

- better define roles and responsibilities of all key CNCI participants, such as the National Cyber Security Center, to ensure that essential governmentwide cybersecurity activities are fully coordinated;
- establish measures to determine the effectiveness of CNCI projects in making federal information systems more secure and track progress against those measures;
- establish an appropriate level of transparency about CNCI by clarifying the rationale for classifying information, ensuring that as much information is made public as is appropriate, and providing justification for withholding information from the public;
- establish a coordinated approach for the federal government in conducting international outreach to address cyber security issues strategically;
- establish a strategic approach to identity management and authentication, linked to HSPD-12 implementation, to provide greater assurance that only authorized individuals and other entities can gain access to federal information systems; and
- reach agreement on the scope of CNCI's education projects to ensure that an adequate cadre of skilled personnel is developed to protect federal information systems.

45

Agency Comments and Our Evaluation

We provided a draft of this briefing to OMB, ODNI, and the Department of State for review and comment. In comments provided via e-mail, an official in OMB's Office of E-Government and Information Technology agreed that federal cybersecurity policy has many areas that could use improvement but disagreed that these issues are all related to CNCI, noting that the CNCI was built upon existing cybersecurity activities within the federal government and did not eliminate or subsume other activities. We agree that CNCI was not intended to subsume all federal activities related to cybersecurity and have clarified our briefing to avoid a potential misunderstanding. Nevertheless, we believe that the challenges we identified remain of critical importance in determining whether CNCI can achieve its objectives related to securing federal information systems.

Regarding our briefing's discussion of the need to better define roles and responsibilities of federal entities in securing federal systems, OMB observed that specific roles and responsibilities for the various CNCI initiatives were clearly defined. We agree that, as described in our briefing, lead responsibility has been assigned for each of the CNCI initiatives. However, this observation does not diminish the larger challenge that CNCI faces in better establishing federal cybersecurity roles and responsibilities. For example, we note that, according to the then-acting director, the NCSC has not been fully operational and has had unclear responsibilities. OMB commented that NCSC's responsibilities would not overlap with other federal entities involved in incident detection and response; however, we disagree. US-CERT, for example, which handles incident response, engages in extensive cross-agency coordination, and it remains unclear how this function differs from the responsibilities planned for NCSC.

46

Agency Comments and Our Evaluation

Regarding international outreach, OMB noted that a formal "deconfliction" process exists among federal agencies regarding international issues. However, the challenge we identified is a larger issue, involving establishing a coordinated strategy among federal agencies, something that has not been undertaken as part of CNCI and that remains critical to its success.

Similarly, with regard to identity management and authentication, OMB stated the CNCI did not address this topic because it relied on the implementation of Homeland Security Presidential Directive 12 (HSPD-12). We disagree. The briefing acknowledges and discusses the role of HSPD-12 and notes that the CSIS commission and the White House Policy Review both agreed that further improvements were needed in this area.

OMB also provided technical comments that we have addressed as appropriate in the final briefing.

47

Agency Comments and Our Evaluation

The Director of Legislative Affairs of ODNI provided written comments on a draft of the briefing. In its comments, ODNI agreed that the challenges we identified should have been included or accounted for in CNCI but raised concern that the program should not be criticized for items that were not included in it. As previously stated, we agree that CNCI was not intended to subsume all federal activities related to cybersecurity and have clarified our briefing to avoid a potential misunderstanding. Nevertheless, we believe that the challenges we identified remain of critical importance in determining whether CNCI can achieve its objectives related to securing federal information systems. In addition, ODNI provided comments that were technical in nature, which we have addressed, as appropriate, in the final briefing.

The Director of the Office of Computer Security at the Department of State provided technical comments via e-mail that we have addressed as appropriate in the final briefing.

48

Appendix II: Comments from the Office of Management and Budget

EXECUTIVE OFFICE OF THE PRESIDENT
OFFICE OF MANAGEMENT AND BUDGET
WASHINGTON, D.C. 20503

Gregory Wilshusen
Director
The Government Accountability Office
441 G Street, Northwest
Washington, D.C. 20548

Dear Mr. Wilshusen:

Thank you for the opportunity to comment on your draft report, "CYBERSECURITY: Progress Made but Challenges Remain in Defining and Coordinating the Comprehensive National Initiative" (GAO-10-338). We appreciate the work that the Government Accountability Office (GAO) has done in this area and we welcome GAO's interest in this area.

The Comprehensive National Cybersecurity Initiative (CNCI), created by National Security Presidential Directive 54/Homeland Security Presidential Directive 23 (NSPD-54/HSPD-23), is a set of 12 discrete activities that were designed to coordinate with other existing Federal cybersecurity activities to protect the Federal Executive Branch agencies and departments from specific threats. The value of the CNCI was reinforced in the President's *Cyberspace Policy Review*.

As we explained in the technical comments that we provided to GAO staff on October 29, 2009, we do not concur with some of the findings, conclusions and recommendations in the report.

Findings and Conclusions:

With respect to the findings and conclusions made by GAO concerning better defining roles and responsibilities for agencies participating in the CNCI, we do not concur. The roles and responsibilities of agencies participating in the CNCI are clearly defined by NSPD-54/HSPD-23. For example, as illustrated in Table 1 in your report, lead agencies have been designated for each initiative. Lead agencies are held to implementation plans and report quarterly on their progress against goals.

In addition, the draft report cites the agencies' response to the July 2009 distributed denial of service attacks against some federal websites as an example of the confusion over roles and responsibilities for agencies participating in the CNCI. As we explained in the technical comments that we provided to GAO staff on October 29, 2009, the government's response to the incident was not an activity that fell under the roles and responsibilities under CNCI. Operational incident response management for civil executive branch departments and agencies is set forth in the Federal Information Security Management Act.

The draft report also states the view that there are "overlapping and uncoordinated" responsibilities regarding cyber information sharing and situational awareness. We do not agree. The National Computer Security Center is responsible for assisting with situational awareness across the government, public and private sectors. As the draft report notes, the other cyber security response centers are responsible for operational incident response.

The draft report also states the view that the role of the NCSC is unclear. We do not agree. As we explained in the technical comments we provided to GAO staff on October 29, 2009, NCSC coordinates incident information flowing between multiple operational incident response centers in the Federal Government. It does not handle incident detection and response, which is a responsibility of operational incident response centers. NCSC's role was predicated on the implementation of the activities in initiative 5: Connecting the Centers. As these activities have been delayed, the implementation of the NCSC has also been delayed.

Finally, as we explained in the technical comments we provided to GAO staff on October 29, 2009, we also requested that you clarify the description of the interagency policy committee (IPC) to explain that IPCs are formal bodies that deal with interagency coordination in many areas. The IPC, in this case, operates under the National Security Council which is the advising and consenting party to NSPD-54/HSPD-23. IPCs are components of a decision structure established by Presidential Directive that includes both deputies and principals of agencies.

Recommendations:

Of the six recommendations that GAO makes in this report to the Director of the Office of Management and Budget, we do not concur with one and concur with five. We do not concur with the recommendation to better define roles and responsibilities of all key CNCI participants since, NSPD-54/HSPD-23 clearly defines roles and responsibilities for activities within the CNCI.

We concur with the recommendations related to the CNCI with the following comments:

1. *Recommendation: establish measures to determine the effectiveness of CNCI projects in making federal information systems more secure and track progress against those measures.*
   Comment: As we explained in the technical comments we provided to GAO staff on October 29, 2009, establishment of performance measures has always been part of the planning for the CNCI once the initiatives were past the implementation stage.

2. *Recommendation: establish an appropriate level of transparency about CNCI by clarifying the rationale for classifying information, ensuring that as much information is made public as is appropriate, and providing justification for withholding information from the public.*
   Comment: Consideration of the classification of information about the CNCI is already being done by the IPC responsible for CNCI oversight. We believe that is the correct venue for this activity.

3. *Recommendation: reach agreement on the scope of CNCI's education projects to ensure that an adequate cadre of skilled personnel is developed to protect federal information systems.*
   Comment: The IPC responsible for CNCI oversight has already completed a re-evaluation of the CNCI's education projects and has redefined their scope. We believe that the IPC is the correct and appropriate venue for this activity.

We concur with the two recommendations that are related to strategic challenges in areas that are not part of the CNCI with the following comments:

1. *Recommendation: establish a coordinated approach for the federal government in conducting international outreach to address cybersecurity issues strategically.*
   Comment: This activity is already in existence within the appropriate IPC under the National Security Staff. We believe that this is the correct and appropriate venue for this activity.

2. *Recommendation: continue development of a strategic approach to identity management and authentication, linked to HSPD-12 authentication, as initially described in the CIO Council's plan for implementing federal identity, credential, and access management so as to provide greater assurance that only authorized individuals and entities can gain access to federal systems.*
   Comment: Such a strategic approach already exists in The Federal Identity, Credential, and Access Management (FICAM) Roadmap and Implementation Guidance, dated November 10, 2009. This document provides architecture and implementation guidance to agencies in implementing Federal identity management requirements.

The security of Federal information systems is a major concern of this Administration. Our nation's security and economic prosperity depend on the stability and integrity of our Federal communications and information infrastructure. Recognizing the challenges and opportunities, the President identified cybersecurity as one of the top priorities of his administration and directed a 60-day comprehensive review to assess U.S. polices and structures for cybersecurity. The President has also appointed Howard Schmidt as the Special Assistance to the President and Cybersecurity Coordinator to increase and sustain attention to cybersecurity.

Thank you again for the opportunity to comment on this draft report.

Sincerely,

Vivek Kundra
Federal Chief Information Officer

Appendix III: Comments from the Office of the Director of National Intelligence

Note: GAO comments regarding this letter appear at the end of this appendix.

UNCLASSIFIED

OFFICE OF THE DIRECTOR OF NATIONAL INTELLIGENCE
WASHINGTON, DC 20511

JAN 22 2010

Mr. Gregory C. Wilshusen
Director, Information Security Issues
United States Government
Accountability Office
Washington, DC 20548

Dear Mr. Wilshusen:

(U) This responds to your request dated 30 Dec. 2009, for review of a draft GAO report, "CYBERSECURITY: Progress Made but Challenges Remain in Defining and Coordinating the Comprehensive National Initiative", GAO 10-338, dated February 2010. This report relates to an inquiry originally initiated in February, 2009 on the Comprehensive National Cybersecurity Initiative (GAO Code 311019) by Ms. Janet A. St. Laurent, Managing Director, Defense Capabilities and Management United States Government Accountability Office.

See comment 1.

(U) This office provided a detailed review of the body of this report on 4 November, 2009, under GAO Code 31101. Those recommendations remain largely unincorporated in this product. As a result, the concerns expressed in that communication remain and carry forward to this product as well. I request that your office refer back to those comments, incorporate them fully and adjust the report accordingly.

(U) If you have any questions regarding this matter, please do not hesitate to contact me at (703) 275-2473.

Sincerely,

for Kathleen Turner
Director of Legislative Affairs

UNCLASSIFIED

GAO Comment

1. In its earlier comments, ODNI had raised concern that CNCI should not be criticized for items that were not included in it. As discussed in the letter, to avoid potential misunderstanding, we have clarified that two of the challenges we identified are not connected to specific CNCI projects but rather relate to additional cybersecurity activities that are necessary to achieve CNCI's overall goal of securing federal information systems.

Appendix IV: GAO Contacts and Staff Acknowledgments

GAO Contacts

Gregory C. Wilshusen at (202) 512-6244 or wilshuseng@gao.gov, or Davi M. D'Agostino at (202) 512-5431 or dagostinod@gao.gov.

Staff Acknowledgments

In addition to the individual named above, key contributions to this report were made by John de Ferrari (Assistant Director), Sher`rie Bacon, Matthew Grote, Nick Marinos, Lee McCracken, David Plocher, Daniel Swartz, and Jeffrey Woodward.

GAO's Mission

The Government Accountability Office, the audit, evaluation, and investigative arm of Congress, exists to support Congress in meeting its constitutional responsibilities and to help improve the performance and accountability of the federal government for the American people. GAO examines the use of public funds; evaluates federal programs and policies; and provides analyses, recommendations, and other assistance to help Congress make informed oversight, policy, and funding decisions. GAO's commitment to good government is reflected in its core values of accountability, integrity, and reliability.

Obtaining Copies of GAO Reports and Testimony

The fastest and easiest way to obtain copies of GAO documents at no cost is through GAO's Web site (www.gao.gov). Each weekday afternoon, GAO posts on its Web site newly released reports, testimony, and correspondence. To have GAO e-mail you a list of newly posted products, go to www.gao.gov and select "E-mail Updates."

Order by Phone

The price of each GAO publication reflects GAO's actual cost of production and distribution and depends on the number of pages in the publication and whether the publication is printed in color or black and white. Pricing and ordering information is posted on GAO's Web site, http://www.gao.gov/ordering.htm.

Place orders by calling (202) 512-6000, toll free (866) 801-7077, or TDD (202) 512-2537.

Orders may be paid for using American Express, Discover Card, MasterCard, Visa, check, or money order. Call for additional information.

To Report Fraud, Waste, and Abuse in Federal Programs

Contact:

Web site: www.gao.gov/fraudnet/fraudnet.htm
E-mail: fraudnet@gao.gov
Automated answering system: (800) 424-5454 or (202) 512-7470

Congressional Relations

Ralph Dawn, Managing Director, dawnr@gao.gov, (202) 512-4400
U.S. Government Accountability Office, 441 G Street NW, Room 7125
Washington, DC 20548

Public Affairs

Chuck Young, Managing Director, youngc1@gao.gov, (202) 512-4800
U.S. Government Accountability Office, 441 G Street NW, Room 7149
Washington, DC 20548

www.ingramcontent.com/pod-product-compliance
Lightning Source LLC
Chambersburg PA
CBHW082112070326
40689CB00052B/4614

* 9 7 8 1 4 8 2 3 8 3 9 6 6 *